DANIIL KARABUT

The History of Street Art

From the Underground to the Mainstream

"Art is not what you see, but what you make others see."

Edgar Degas

Contents

Foreword

Street art is a unique and powerful art form that has been shaping our cities and communities for decades. From its origins in the underground graffiti scene to its current place in the mainstream art world, street art has evolved into a dynamic and multifaceted art form that engages with a wide range of social, political, and cultural issues.

In this book, we explore the rich history of street art, from its early beginnings in the countercultural movements of the 1960s and 1970s, to its current place in the art world. We will look at the different forms of street art, including tags, graffiti, murals, and stencil art, and explore how street art has been used to address a wide range of social and political issues.

We will also examine some of the controversies and challenges surrounding street art, including questions around ownership, authenticity, and commercialization. Through it all, we will see how street art has become a powerful tool for social and political engagement, giving voice to those who are often marginalized or silenced in mainstream society.

As we journey through the rich and varied history of street art, we will also explore how digital technologies are shaping the future of street art, allowing artists to create new forms of art and engage with audiences around the world.

Whether you are a longtime street art enthusiast or a new-comer to this vibrant and dynamic art form, this book is for you. Through the power of street art, we can transform public spaces, create new opportunities for community engagement and dialogue, and challenge dominant narratives and power structures. Join us on this journey and discover the power of street art for yourself.

Preface

Street art is a form of artistic expression that has fascinated me for many years. From the bold tags and murals that adorn the walls of our cities, to the intricate stencil works and political statements that challenge our assumptions and beliefs, street art has become a powerful force for social and political change in communities around the world.

This book is the culmination of years of research and exploration into the rich and varied history of street art. Through it, I hope to provide readers with an introduction to this dynamic and multifaceted art form, and to explore its many facets and dimensions.

Throughout the book, we will explore the history of street art, from its early beginnings in the underground graffiti scene to its current place in the mainstream art world. We will look at the different forms of street art, from tags and graffiti to murals and installations, and explore how street art has been used to address a wide range of social and political issues.

We will also examine some of the controversies and challenges surrounding street art, including questions around ownership, authenticity, and commercialization. Through it all, we will see how street art has become a powerful tool for social and political engagement, giving voice to those who are often marginalized or silenced in mainstream society.

As we journey through the rich and varied history of street art, we will also explore how digital technologies are shaping the future of street art, allowing artists to create new forms of art and engage with audiences around the world.

I hope that this book will inspire readers to engage with street art in new and exciting ways, and to see the world in a different light. Street art has the power to transform public spaces, spark important conversations, and create a more just and equitable world for us all. So join me on this journey through the history of street art, and discover the power and potential of this vibrant and dynamic art form.

Acknowledgement

Writing this book has been a labor of love, and I could not have done it without the help and support of many people. First and foremost, I would like to thank the street artists who have inspired me with their creativity, passion, and commitment to social and political change. Your works have challenged me to see the world in new and exciting ways, and have given voice to those who are often silenced or marginalized in mainstream society.

I would also like to thank the scholars and activists who have contributed to the ongoing evolution of street art, and who have provided invaluable insights and perspectives throughout the writing of this book. Your research and activism have helped to shape the field of street art, and your passion and dedication have inspired me to continue to explore this dynamic and multifaceted art form.

I am also grateful to the museums, galleries, and art institutions around the world who have hosted exhibitions of street art, and who have helped to legitimize street art as a form of art in its own right. Your recognition and support have helped to bring street art to a wider audience, and have helped to spark important conversations around the social and political issues that street art engages with.

Finally, I would like to thank my family and friends for their love and support throughout the writing of this book. Your encouragement, feedback, and patience have been invaluable, and I could not have done this without you.

Thank you all for your contributions to this book, and for your ongoing commitment to the power and potential of street art.

Chapter 1: Origins of Street Art

Street art has a long and varied history, with roots that can be traced back to the earliest forms of human expression. Ancient cultures around the world left their marks on rocks, cave walls, and other surfaces, creating images that were often linked to ritual, myth, and identity.

Fast forward to the 20th century, and we see the emergence of modern street art in the 1960s and 70s, as disenfranchised youth in urban areas such as New York City and Philadelphia began to use graffiti as a form of artistic expression.

In the early days, graffiti was a crude and basic form of tagging, where writers would use spray paint and markers to create simple, often illegible tags on walls, trains, and other public surfaces. However, as the graffiti subculture grew and evolved, writers began to develop new techniques, styles, and codes to communicate with each other and express their identities.

One of the key elements of early graffiti was its emphasis on anonymity and secrecy. Graffiti writers often adopted pseudonyms, or "tags," and used them to mark their presence in public spaces. They also developed their own codes and symbols, which could be used to convey complex messages and information to other writers.

Graffiti soon became associated with rebellion and resistance, as marginalized youth used it to assert their presence and challenge authority. In some cases, graffiti was also used to protest against social and political injustices, with writers using their work to make bold statements about issues such as racism, poverty, and inequality.

By the 1980s, graffiti had become a global phenomenon, spreading to cities around the world and inspiring new forms of street art. From the early days of crude tagging, street art had evolved into a more complex and varied art form, with artists using a wide range of techniques, materials, and styles to create works that were both visually striking and socially meaningful.

In the next chapters of this book, we will explore the evolution of street art from its origins as a subversive, often illegal activity to its current status as a legitimate art form that is recognized and celebrated around the world. We will examine the various styles and techniques that have emerged in street art over time, as well as the social and cultural context in which these works were created. We will also look at the impact that street art has had on urban spaces and communities, and how it has transformed our understanding of art and public space.

Chapter 2: Graffiti as a Form of Rebellion

In the early days of street art, graffiti was seen as a form of rebellion against authority, an expression of defiance and resistance by those who felt marginalized and excluded from mainstream society. Graffiti writers used the city's walls, trains, and other public surfaces as their canvas, reclaiming these spaces as a means of self-expression and creative assertion.

One of the key features of early graffiti was its focus on individualism and identity. Graffiti writers often used their tags to create a sense of identity and belonging within the subculture, while at the same time distancing themselves from the mainstream. They also used graffiti to assert their presence in public space, claiming these spaces as their own and challenging the authority of those who sought to control them.

However, as graffiti became more widespread and visible, it also became more controversial. Many people viewed graffiti as a form of vandalism, a destructive act that defaced public property and caused economic harm to businesses and communities. In response, authorities began to crack down on graffiti, enforcing stricter laws and penalties against those caught in the act.

Despite this, graffiti continued to flourish as a form of creative expression, with writers using new techniques and styles to push the boundaries of what was possible in the medium. Writers also began to organize themselves into crews, working together to create larger and more complex pieces that would be visible to a wider audience.

In the 1980s, graffiti began to influence popular culture, with elements of graffiti and street art appearing in music videos, fashion, and advertising. This helped to raise the profile of graffiti and street art, bringing it to the attention of a wider audience and helping to legitimize it as a form of art.

Chapter 3: The Evolution of Graffiti Writing

Graffiti writing has a rich and diverse history that spans several decades and has influenced the development of street art as a whole. In this chapter, we will explore how graffiti writers developed new techniques, styles, and codes to communicate with each other and express their identities.

In the early days of graffiti, writers used simple tags or "throw-ups" - quickly sprayed names or symbols that were meant to be easily recognizable. However, as the subculture grew and became more competitive, writers began to develop more elaborate styles that would set them apart from others.

One of the key developments in graffiti writing was the invention of the "wildstyle," a complex and highly stylized form of writing that featured intricate lettering and designs. Wildstyle writing was often difficult to read and understand, which made it more challenging for authorities to crack down on graffiti writers.

Another important development in graffiti writing was the creation of "bubble letters," which were larger and rounder than traditional graffiti letters. This made them more visible and legible, and they soon became popular among writers who wanted their tags to be easily recognizable.

As graffiti writing evolved, writers also developed their own codes and symbols, which were used to convey complex messages and information to other writers. These codes included "hand styles," which were unique signatures that writers used to sign their work, and "burners," which were highly detailed and colorful pieces that required more time and skill to create.

Graffiti writing also influenced the development of other street art techniques, such as stencil art and wheatpasting. Stencils, which are pre-made designs that can be quickly sprayed onto a surface, were initially used by graffiti writers to create complex and detailed images. Wheatpasting, which involves pasting pre-made images onto surfaces using a mixture of water and wheat paste, allowed artists to create larger and more detailed works that could be produced quickly and easily.

Chapter 4: Street Art Goes Global

Street art has become a global phenomenon, with artists in cities around the world using public space as a canvas to create works that are visually striking and socially meaningful. In this chapter, we will explore how street art has evolved and spread to different parts of the world, and how local contexts and cultures have influenced the art form.

One of the key features of street art is its ability to reflect and respond to the social and cultural issues of the communities in which it is created. In many cities, street art has emerged as a form of protest against the social and economic injustices that affect marginalized communities. In other cities, street art has become a way for artists to engage with their surroundings and transform neglected or forgotten spaces into vibrant and meaningful places.

Street art has also been shaped by local artistic traditions and cultural contexts. In Latin America, for example, street art has been influenced by the region's long history of muralism, with artists using large-scale murals to create works that celebrate the region's indigenous cultures and challenge political oppression. In Africa, street art has been used to address issues such as poverty, HIV/AIDS, and political corruption, while also celebrating the continent's rich cultural heritage.

In Europe, street art has become a prominent part of the urban landscape, with cities such as London, Paris, and Berlin featuring a diverse range of street art styles and techniques. Street artists in these cities have used their work to comment on issues such as gentrification, consumerism, and political extremism, while also exploring new forms of public engagement and collaboration.

Street art has also spread to other parts of the world, including Asia, Australia, and the Middle East, where artists are using their work to address a range of social and political issues. In China, for example, street art has become a way for artists to challenge the country's strict censorship laws and assert their creative freedom.

Chapter 5: The Rise of Stencil Art

Stencil art has become a popular form of street art, with artists using pre-made stencils to create bold and striking images that often convey powerful political and social commentary. In this chapter, we will explore the origins of stencil art, and how it has become a prominent part of the street art landscape.

The use of stencils in street art can be traced back to the early days of graffiti, when writers would use stencils to quickly create complex and detailed images. However, stencil art as we know it today emerged in the late 1970s and early 1980s, with artists such as Blek le Rat and Banksy popularizing the use of stencils in street art.

One of the key advantages of stencils is their versatility and ease of use. Stencils can be quickly and easily applied to a surface using spray paint, which allows artists to produce large-scale images with minimal effort. Stencils also allow artists to create highly detailed and intricate images, which can be difficult to achieve using freehand techniques.

Stencil art has been used to address a wide range of social and political issues, including poverty, war, and environmental degradation. Stencil artists often use images and symbols that are immediately recognizable to viewers, such as political leaders or corporate logos, to create works that are both visually striking and socially meaningful.

Stencil art has also been embraced by mainstream culture, with artists such as Banksy achieving global fame and recognition for their work. Stencil art has been exhibited in galleries and museums around the world, and collectors have paid top dollar for stencil art pieces.

However, stencil art has also faced controversy and criticism, particularly from those who view it as a form of vandalism or as lacking in artistic merit. Some artists have also criticized stencil art for being too easy and formulaic, and for not being sufficiently connected to the communities in which it is created.

Chapter 6: Murals and Public Art

Street artists have long used murals and other forms of public art to transform urban landscapes and engage with communities. In this chapter, we will explore the different ways in which street artists have used murals and public art to create works that are both visually striking and socially meaningful.

Murals are large-scale works of art that are painted directly onto a surface, often a building or a wall. Murals have been used for centuries to decorate public spaces and convey messages to viewers, and they have become an important part of the street art landscape.

Street artists have used murals to address a wide range of social and political issues, from climate change to gentrification to police brutality. Murals are often created in collaboration with community members, and they can help to foster a sense of pride and ownership in the neighborhoods where they are located.

Public art can take many forms beyond murals, such as sculptures, installations, and performances. Like murals, public art can transform public spaces and create new opportunities for community engagement and dialogue.

One of the advantages of public art is its ability to reach a wide audience, beyond those who might typically visit galleries or museums. Public art can be enjoyed by anyone who passes by, and it can help to create a sense of connection and community in public spaces.

However, public art can also be controversial, particularly if it addresses sensitive or controversial issues. Some artists have faced criticism and even legal action for their public art projects, which have been seen as provocative or offensive by some members of the community.

Despite these challenges, many street artists continue to use murals and public art as a means of creating positive change and empowering communities. In the next chapter of this book, we will explore how street art has gained greater recognition and legitimacy as a form of art, and how museums and galleries have exhibited the work of street artists.

Chapter 7: Street Art Enters the Mainstream

Street art has gained greater recognition and legitimacy as a form of art in recent years, with museums and galleries around the world exhibiting the work of street artists. In this chapter, we will explore how street art has entered the mainstream, and how this has impacted the art form.

One of the key drivers of street art's mainstream success has been the emergence of high-profile street artists such as Banksy and Shepard Fairey. These artists have achieved global recognition and acclaim for their work, and have helped to legitimize street art as a form of art that is worthy of critical attention and analysis.

Museums and galleries have also played an important role in bringing street art to a wider audience. In recent years, major museums such as the Museum of Contemporary Art in Los Angeles and the Tate Modern in London have hosted exhibitions of street art, featuring works by both established and emerging artists.

The mainstreaming of street art has also led to increased commercialization, with street art becoming a popular subject for advertising campaigns and corporate branding. Some street artists have even partnered with brands to create works that are intended to promote products or services.

This commercialization has raised concerns among some street artists, who view it as a form of co-optation and exploitation. Some artists feel that their work has been appropriated and used for profit without their consent, while others worry that the mainstreaming of street art will lead to a loss of its rebellious and subversive spirit.

Despite these concerns, many street artists continue to create works that are socially and politically engaged, using public space as a means of addressing important issues and challenging dominant narratives. The mainstreaming of street art has given these artists a wider platform and greater exposure, allowing their work to reach new audiences and have a greater impact.

Chapter 8: The Politics of Street Art

Street art has always been a politically charged art form, reflecting the social and political issues of the communities where it is created. In this chapter, we will explore how street art has been used as a tool for political activism and protest, and how it has challenged dominant narratives and power structures.

Street art has been used to address a wide range of political issues, including inequality, police brutality, environmental degradation, and human rights abuses. Street artists often use their work to challenge dominant narratives and to give voice to those who are marginalized or oppressed.

One of the key strengths of street art is its ability to engage with audiences in public spaces, creating a sense of dialogue and engagement that is often lacking in traditional forms of political activism. Street art can also reach a wider audience than traditional forms of political activism, such as protests or rallies, and can create a lasting impact on the communities where it is located.

Street art has also been used as a form of political resistance in countries where freedom of expression is limited or non-existent. In these contexts, street artists often risk arrest, imprisonment, or even violence for their work, making street art a powerful tool for political dissent and resistance.

However, street art's political engagement has also faced criticism and opposition, particularly from those who view it as a form of vandalism or a threat to public safety. Some authorities have sought to regulate or even ban street art, arguing that it is a form of illegal activity that undermines the authority of the state.

Despite these challenges, street art continues to be an important tool for political engagement and protest, giving voice to those who are often marginalized or silenced in mainstream society.

Chapter 9: Street Art and the Digital Age

The rise of digital technologies has had a profound impact on the art world, and street art is no exception. In this chapter, we will explore how street artists have embraced digital tools and platforms to create new forms of street art and engage with audiences around the world.

Digital technologies have opened up new possibilities for street artists, allowing them to create works that are more complex, interactive, and responsive than traditional street art. Augmented reality, for example, allows street artists to create virtual artworks that can be viewed through a smartphone or tablet, while 3D printing allows artists to create sculptures and installations that would be difficult or impossible to produce using traditional techniques.

Social media has also played an important role in the evolution of street art, allowing artists to share their work with a global audience and to connect with other artists and activists around the world. Platforms such as Instagram and Twitter have become important tools for street artists to promote their work and to engage with their followers, while also building a sense of community and collaboration.

Digital technologies have also raised new questions and challenges for street art, particularly around issues of ownership, authenticity, and commercialization. Some artists have expressed concern that the ease with which digital images can be copied and distributed online undermines the value and integrity of their work, while others worry that digital technologies will lead to the further commodification of street art.

Despite these challenges, many street artists continue to embrace digital technologies as a means of expanding the reach and impact of their work. Digital tools and platforms have allowed street artists to engage with new audiences and to create works that are more interactive and responsive to their surroundings, pushing the boundaries of what street art can be.

In the final chapter of this book, we will reflect on the impact of street art on society and on the art world, and explore what the future may hold for this dynamic and continually evolving art form in the digital age.

Chapter 10: The Future of Street Art

Street art has come a long way since its origins in the 1960s and 1970s, evolving into a dynamic and multifaceted art form that engages with a wide range of social, political, and cultural issues. In this final chapter, we will reflect on the history of street art and explore what the future may hold for this continually evolving art form.

One of the key trends shaping the future of street art is the increasing use of technology, as artists embrace digital tools and platforms to create new forms of street art and engage with audiences around the world. Augmented reality, 3D printing, and other digital technologies are likely to become even more prevalent in street art in the coming years, allowing artists to create works that are more interactive, responsive, and immersive.

Another important trend is the growing recognition and legitimacy of street art as a form of art in its own right. Major museums and galleries around the world have hosted exhibitions of street art, and collectors and art buyers have shown a growing interest in acquiring street art pieces. This trend is likely to continue, as street art gains greater recognition and acceptance in the art world.

However, street art's continued evolution and growth is not

without challenges. Issues such as ownership, authenticity, and commercialization remain important concerns for street artists, and questions around the relationship between street art and public space are likely to become even more pressing as street art becomes more mainstream.

Despite these challenges, street art is likely to continue to be a powerful tool for social and political engagement, allowing artists to challenge dominant narratives and give voice to those who are often marginalized or silenced in mainstream society. Street art has the potential to transform public spaces, create new opportunities for community engagement and dialogue, and spark important conversations around some of the most pressing issues of our time.

As street art continues to evolve and adapt to new technologies and changing social and political landscapes, one thing is clear: it will continue to be a vibrant and important part of the art world, and a powerful force for positive change in communities around the world.

Conclusion

Street art is a dynamic and continually evolving art form that has its roots in the countercultural movements of the 1960s and 1970s. Since then, street art has grown and evolved, becoming a powerful tool for social and political engagement, and a vibrant part of the art world.

Throughout this book, we have explored the history of street art, from its origins in the underground graffiti scene to its current place in the mainstream. We have looked at the different forms of street art, including tags, graffiti, murals, and stencil art, and explored how street art has been used to address a wide range of social, political, and cultural issues.

We have also examined some of the challenges and controversies surrounding street art, including questions around ownership, authenticity, and commercialization, and looked at how street artists have used digital technologies to create new forms of street art and engage with audiences around the world.

Despite these challenges, street art continues to be a powerful force for positive change in communities around the world. Street art has the potential to transform public spaces, create new opportunities for community engagement and dialogue, and challenge dominant narratives and power structures.

As street art continues to evolve and adapt to new technologies and changing social and political landscapes, it is clear that it will continue to be an important and vibrant part of the art world. Whether it takes the form of a simple tag on a wall or a complex augmented reality installation, street art will continue to be a powerful tool for social and political engagement, and a force for positive change in the world.

Afterword

As I conclude this book, I am struck by the incredible diversity and creativity of the street art scene. From the bold tags and colorful murals that adorn our city walls, to the intricate stencil works and powerful political statements that challenge our assumptions and beliefs, street art is an ever-changing and dynamic art form that speaks to us in a myriad of ways.

Throughout the writing of this book, I have been continually inspired by the ingenuity and passion of the street artists I have encountered. Their works have opened my eyes to new ways of seeing the world, and have challenged me to question my own assumptions and biases.

I hope that this book has served as an introduction to the rich and varied world of street art, and that it has inspired readers to seek out and engage with this vibrant and powerful art form. Whether you are a seasoned art lover or a newcomer to the world of street art, there is always something new to discover and explore.

I would like to express my deepest gratitude to all the street artists, activists, and scholars who have contributed to the ongoing evolution of street art. Your creativity, passion, and commitment to social and political change are an inspiration to us all.

Finally, I would like to thank you, the reader, for embarking on this journey with me. I hope that this book has provided you with a deeper understanding and appreciation of the rich and complex history of street art, and that it has inspired you to engage with this important and dynamic art form in new and exciting ways.

www.ingramcontent.com/pod-product-compliance
Lightning Source LLC
Chambersburg PA
CBHW071124220526
45467CB00004B/2041